ROYAL COURT

The Royal Court Theatre presents

CIRCLE MIRROR TRANSFORMATION
by **Annie Baker**

CIRCLE MIRROR TRANSFORMATION was first performed at The Rose Lipman Building, Haggerston, on Friday 5th July 2013 as part of the Theatre Local season.

Playwrights Horizons, Inc., New York City, produced the World Premiere of CIRCLE MIRROR TRANSFORMATION Off-Broadway in 2009.

CIRCLE MIRROR TRANSFORMATION was developed, in part, with the assistance of the Sundance Institute Theatre Program, with additional support from the Sundance Institute's Time Warner Storytelling Fellowship.

CIRCLE MIRROR TRANSFORMATION

by Annie Baker

Marty **Imelda Staunton**
James **Danny Webb**
Schultz **Toby Jones**
Theresa **Fenella Woolgar**
Lauren **Shannon Tarbet**

Director **James Macdonald**
Designer **Chloe Lamford**
Lighting Designer **Peter Mumford**
Sound Designer **Carolyn Downing**
Casting Director **Amy Ball**
Production Manager **Niall Black**
Stage Managers **Fiona Kennedy** & **Joni Carter**
Stage Management Work Placement **TJ Chappell**
Costume Supervisor **Iona Kenrick** & **Jackie Orton**
Dialect Coach **Penny Dyer**

The Royal Court & Stage Management wish to thank the following for their help with this production:
Anna the Hulagan, The Mill Co. Project, Create London.

THE COMPANY

ANNIE BAKER (Writer)

PLAYS INCLUDE: The Flick, Circle Mirror Transformation (Playwrights Horizons); The Aliens (Rattlestick Playwrights Theater/The Bush); Body Awareness (Atlantic Theater Company); Uncle Vanya (adaptation & costume design: Soho Rep).

AWARDS INCLUDE: The Susan Smith Blackburn Prize & Obie Award for Excellence in Playwriting (The Flick); Obie Award for Best New American Play (Circle Mirror Transformation); Obie Award for Best New American Play (The Aliens); New York Drama Critics Circle Emerging Talent Award & a Lilly Award for Playwriting.

CAROLYN DOWNING (Sound Designer)

FOR THE ROYAL COURT: The Low Road, Choir Boy, The Witness, Our Private Life, Oxford Street, Alaska.

OTHER THEATRE/OPERA INCLUDES: Chimerica, Blood Wedding (Almeida); Fanny och Alexander (Malmö Stadsteater); Love Song, Little Dogs (Frantic Assembly); Beautiful Burnout (Frantic Assembly/National Theatre of Scotland); Double Feature (National); King John, The Gods Weep, The Winter's Tale, Pericles, Days of Significance (RSC); Lower Ninth, Dimetos, Absurdia (Donmar); Angels in America, Millennium Approaches, Perestroika (Headlong); After Dido (ENO); Amerika, Krieg der Bilder (Staatstheater Mainz); All My Sons (Broadway); Tre Kroner - Gustav III (Dramaten, Stockholm); Blackta, After Miss Julie, Ghosts, Dirty Butterfly (Young Vic); To Kill A Mockingbird, The Country Wife, A Whistle In The Dark, Moonshed (Royal Exchange, Manchester); Lulu, The Kreutzer Sonata, Vanya, State Of Emergency, The Internationalist (Gate); Andersen's English, Flight Path (Out Of Joint); Gambling (Soho); Belongings (Hampstead); The Water Engine (503/Young Vic); Stallerhof, No Way Out (Southwark); After Miss Julie, Othello (Salisbury); The Watery Part of the World (Sound & Fury); Gone To Earth (Shared Experience); 3rd Ring Out (Metis Arts).

TOBY JONES (Schultz)

FOR THE ROYAL COURT: Shoot/Get Treasure/Repeat.

OTHER THEATRE INCLUDES: The Painter (Arcola); Every Good Boy Deserves Favour, Measure for Measure (National); Parlour Song (Almeida); The Play What I Wrote (West End/Broadway).

TELEVISION INCLUDES: The Girl, Christopher & His Kind, Mo.

FILM INCLUDES: Serena, Leave to Remain, Winter Soldier, Tinker Tailor Soldier Spy, Berberian Sound Studio, Hunger Games, Red Lights, My Week With Marilyn, Captain America, The Rite, Harry Potter & the Deathly Hallows, The Adventures of Tintin, What's Wrong with Virginia, Sex, Drugs & Rock n Roll, Creation, W, Frost/Nixon, City of Ember, The Mist, Infamous, The Painted Veil.

CHLOE LAMFORD (Designer)

FOR THE ROYAL COURT: Open Court Festival.

OTHER THEATRE INCLUDES: Cannibals (Royal Exchange, Manchester); The History Boys (Sheffield Theatres); 1984 (Headlong); Praxis Makes Perfect, The Radicalisation of Bradley Manning (National Theatre of Wales); Salt, Root & Roe (West End); An Appointment with the Wicker Man, Knives in Hens (National Theatre of Scotland); Let's Make an Opera (Malmo, Sweden); Blackta (costume design), Disco Pigs, Sus (Young Vic); On the Record (Ice & Fire); Rhetoric (Greyscale/Almeida); Small Miracle (Tricycle/Mercury Theatre, Colchester), Brittanicus (Wilton's); Desire Lines (Sherman); This Wide Night (Soho); Joseph K, The Kreutzer Sonata (The Gate); Daisy Pulls it Off (Watermill); My Romantic History (Traverse/Bush/Sheffield Theatres/Birmingham Rep); It Felt Empty When the Heart Went At First But It Is Alright Now, This Wide Night (Clean Break/Soho).

OPERA INCLUDES: The Little Sweep/Let's Make an Opera (Malmo Opera, Sweden); Orpheus in the Underworld, The Cunning Little Vixen (Royal College of Music); War & Peace (Scottish Opera); The Magic Flute (ETO).

AWARDS INCLUDE: TMA Theatre Design Award (Small Miracle). Chloe is the current Arts Foundation Fellow in Design for Performance.

JAMES MACDONALD (Director)

FOR THE ROYAL COURT: Love & Information, Cock (& Duke Theater, New York), Drunk Enough to Say I Love You?, Dying City, Fewer Emergencies, Lucky Dog, Blood, Blasted, 4.48 Psychosis (& European & US tours), Hard Fruit, Real Classy Affair, Cleansed, Bailegangaire, Harry & Me, Simpatico, Blasted, Peaches, Thyestes, The Terrible Voice of Satan.

OTHER THEATRE INCLUDES: #aiww - The Arrest of Ai Weiwei (Hampstead); And No More Shall We Part (Hampstead/Traverse); King Lear, The Book of Grace, Drunk Enough to Say I Love You? (Public Theater, New York); Top Girls (Broadway/MTC); Dying City (Lincoln Center); A Number (New York Theatre Workshop); A Delicate Balance, Judgment Day, The Triumph of Love (Almeida); John Gabriel Borkman (Abbey, Dublin/Brooklyn Academy of Music); Dido Queen of Carthage, The Hour We Knew Nothing of Each Other, Exiles (National); Glengarry Glen Ross (West End); Troilus und Cressida, Die Kopien (Berlin Schaubühne); 4.48 Psychose (Vienna Burgtheater); The Tempest, Roberto Zucco (RSC); Love's Labour's Lost, Richard II (Royal Exchange, Manchester); The Rivals (Nottingham Playhouse); The Crackwalker (Gate); The Seagull (Sheffield Theatres); Miss Julie (Oldham Coliseum); Juno & the Paycock, Ice Cream & Hot Fudge, Romeo & Juliet, Fool for Love, Savage/Love, Master Harold & the Boys (Contact Theatre); Prem (BAC/Soho Poly).

OPERA INCLUDES: Eugene Onegin, Rigoletto (Welsh National Opera); Die Zauberflöte (Garsington); Wolf Club Village, Night Banquet (Almeida Opera); Oedipus Rex, Survivor from Warsaw (Royal Exchange/Hallé); Lives of the Great Poisoners (Second Stride).

FILM INCLUDES: A Number.

James was an Associate Director of the Royal Court from 1992 – 2006 and a NESTA fellow 2003 – 2006.

PETER MUMFORD (Lighting Designer)

FOR THE ROYAL COURT: In the Republic of Happiness, Love & Information, Jumpy (& West End), Our Private Life, Sucker Punch, Cock, The Seagull, Drunk Enough to Say I Love You?, Dying City (& set design).

OTHER THEATRE INCLUDES: King Kong (Global Creatures/Australia); Old Times, Top Hat, Absent Friends, Much Ado about Nothing, The Lion in Winter, The Misanthrope, An Ideal Husband, Carousel, Fiddler on the Roof, Prick Up Your Ears, A View From the Bridge (West End); The Dark Earth & the Light Sky (Almeida); Heartbreak House (Chichester Festival); Bull, A Taste of Honey, Betrayal (Sheffield Theatres); A Streetcar Named Desire (Guthrie, Minneapolis); Scenes from an Execution, Twelfth Night, All's Well That Ends Well, The Reporter, The Hothouse (National); Set & lighting design for Mojo (Theatre-Rites); The Last of the Duchess (Hampstead); Testament (Dublin Theatre Festival).

OPERA & DANCE INCLUDES: Madame Butterfly, Faust, Carmen, Peter Grimes, 125th Gala (New York Met); Eugene Onegin (LA Opera); The Soldier's Tale & Pierrot Lunaire (Chicago Symphony); Passion (Minnesota Opera); The Damnation of Faust, Lucrezia Borgia, Madam Butterfly, Bluebeard's Castle (ENO); La Cenerentola (Glyndebourne); Carmen (& set design), Petrushka (Scottish Ballet); Faster, E=mc², Take Five (Birmingham Royal Ballet); Il Trovatore (Paris); Fidelio, Two Widows, Don Giovanni, The Ring (Scottish Opera); Midsummer Marriage (Chicago Lyric Opera); Eugene Onegin & The Bartered Bride (ROH).

Peter is directing and designing a concert version of The Ring Cycle for Opera North. Peter co-directed and designed sets and lighting for L'Heure Espagnole and L'Enfant et les sortilèges (Opera Zuid).

AWARDS INCLUDE: Olivier Award for Outstanding Achievement in Dance (The Glass Blew In & Fearful Symmetries); Olivier Award for Best Lighting (The Bacchai); Knight of Illumination Award (Sucker Punch).

IMELDA STAUNTON (Marty)

THEATRE INCLUDES: Sweeney Todd (Chichester Festival/West End); A Delicate Balance, There Came a Gypsy Riding (Almeida); Entertaining Mr Sloane, Calico, Uncle Vanya, Into the Woods (West End); Habeas Corpus (Donmar); Life X 3, The Beggar's Opera, Schweyk in the Second, World War, Guys & Dolls, A Chorus of Disapproval (National); Fair Maid of the West, They Shoot Horses Don't They?, The Wizard of Oz (RSC); It's A Mad World, My Masters (Stratford East); Us Good Girls (Soho Poly); The Corn Is Green (Old Vic); The Lady & the Clarinet (King's Head/Edinburgh Festival); Bold Girls (Hampstead); Slavs (Hampstead/Abbey, Dublin).

TELEVISION INCLUDES: The Girl, Psychoville, Cranford Chronicles, Live! Girls! Present Dogtown, Wind in the Willows, My Family & Other Animals, A Midsummer Night's Dream, Little Britain, Fingersmith, Strange, Family Business, Cambridge Spies, David Copperfield, Is It Legal?, Easy Money, The Singing Detective, The Heat of the Day, Ruth Rendell: Sleeping Life, Yellowbacks, An Englishman's Wife, They Never Slept, Up the Garden Path, A Masculine Ending, If You See God Tell Him, Frank Stubbs II, A Bit of Fry & Laurie, Jackanory: Delilah & the Dishwasher Dogs.

FILM INCLUDES: Maleficent, The Awakening, Another Year, Harry Potter & the Deathly Hallows, Taking Woodstock, Three & Out, A Bunch of Amateurs, Harry Potter & the Order of the Phoenix, How About You, Freedom Writers, Toyman, Vera Drake, Nanny McPhee, Bright Young Things, The Virgin of Liverpool, Blackball, Crush, Rat, Another Life, Shakespeare in Love, Comrades, Antonia & Jane: The Definitive Mid Life Report, Much Ado About Nothing, Deadly Advice, Citizen X, Sense & Sensibility, Peter's Friends, Twelfth Night.

AWARDS INCLUDE: Olivier Award for Best Actress in a Musical (Sweeney Todd); Olivier Award for Best Supporting Actress (A Chorus of Disapproval & The Corn Is Green); Olivier Award for Best Actress in a Musical (Into the Woods). Imelda won over fifteen Best Actress awards for Vera Drake including the Venice Film Festival, European Film, Evening Standard British Film and BAFTA.

SHANNON TARBET (Lauren)

FOR THE ROYAL COURT: Spur of the Moment.

OTHER THEATRE INCLUDES: To Kill a Mockingbird (Royal Exchange, Manchester); Mary Shelley (Shared Experience); Skåne (Hampstead); 66 Books (Bush); The Flooded Grave (Bush/Latitude); Mogadishu (Royal Exchange, Manchester/Lyric Hammersmith).

TELEVISION INCLUDES: Lewis, Inspector George Gently, Monroe, Silk.

FILM INCLUDES: A Promise.

RADIO INCLUDES: Mad Girl, Jess's Story, Skyvers, Mogadishu, All the Blood in My Veins.

AWARDS INCLUDE: Manchester Theatre Award for Best Actress in a Supporting Role (Mogadishu).

DANNY WEBB (James)

FOR THE ROYAL COURT: The Witness, Chicken Soup With Barley, Piano Forte, Trade, Blue Bird, Search & Destroy, Serious Money (& Broadway), Carnival War a Go Hot.

OTHER THEATRE INCLUDES: 13, The Gardens of England, As I Lay Dying, Murderers (National); Blasted, Progress (Lyric, Hammersmith); The Ditch (Hightide); The Philanthropist (Donmar); The Green Man (Plymouth Drum/Bush); Richard III (Crucible/tour); Art, Popcorn, Death & the Maiden (West End); Goldhawk Road, The Nest, California Dog Fight (Bush); Dead Funny (Hampstead/West End); Back up the

Hearse (Hampstead); The Pool of Bethesda (Orange Tree); Hamlet (Old Vic); Night Must Fall (Greenwich).

TELEVISION INCLUDES: Strikeback 3, Above Suspicion, Endeavour, Sherlock, Death In Paradise, Being Human, Tucker, Holby City, Midsomer Murders, Hustle, Landgirls, The Bill, Trinity, Britannia High, Casualty, Most Sincerely, New Tricks, Lark Rise to Candleford, Honest, Bloodlines, Miss Marple, The Bill, The Rise & Fall of Rome, Doctor Who, The Inspector Lynley Mysteries, Nostradamus, Totally Frank, Lewis, Heartbeat, A Touch of Frost, Silent Witness, Waking the Dead, My Family, Uncle Adolf, Murder in Suburbia, Dogma, Pepys, Life Begins, Murder Squad, Henry VIII, Cutting It, The Hound of the Baskervilles, Torch, Outside the Rules, Shackleton, McCready and Daughter, Take Me, The Knock, Harbour Lights, Dalziel & Pascoe, Frenchman's Creek, Venus Hunters, The Jump, Out Of Hours, 2.4 Children, The Cleopatra Files, Disaster at the Mall, King Of Chaos, A Perfect State, True Tilda, Sharman, Murder Most Horrid, Mrs Hartley & the Growth Centre, Our Friends In The North, Cardiac Arrest, A Woman's Guide To Adultery, Comics, Head Hunters, Poirot, Tales Of Sherwood Forest, Intimate Contact.

FILM INCLUDES: A Little Chaos, Locke, The Arbor, Visiting Hours, The Courageous Heart of Irena Sendler, Valkyrie, The Harvester, The Aryan Couple, Stealing Lives, The Upside Of Anger, Family Business, Shiner, In The Name Of Love, Still Crazy, Love & Death On Long Island, True Blue, Alien III, Robin Hood, Henry V, Defence of the Realm, The Kid & the Green Baize Vampire, The Year of the Quiet Sun, The Unapproachable, No Exit.

FENELLA WOOLGAR (Theresa)

FOR THE ROYAL COURT: Motortown.

OTHER THEATRE INCLUDES: Hedda Gabler, The Real Thing (Old Vic); The Veil, Time & the Conways (National); Bronte, A Passage to India (Shared Experience); A Midsummer Night's Dream, As You Like It (Royal Exchange, Manchester); The Miser (Salisbury Playhouse); The Cherry Orchard (Theatre Royal, York); How the Other Half Loves (Palace, Watford); Charlie's Aunt (Sheffield Theatres); Way Up Stream (Derby Playhouse); The Playboy of the Western World (Bristol Old Vic); A Comedy of Errors (Oddsocks Theatre Co.).

TELEVISION INCLUDES: Spies of Warsaw, Case Histories, Silk, Poirot: Halloween Party, Freezing, Doctor Who IV, Jekyll, Mr. Loveday's Little Outing, He Knew He Was Right, Eroica, The Way We Live Now, People Like Us.

FILM INCLUDES: Mike Leigh Untitled 13, St Trinian's, Scoop, Wah Wah, Vera Drake, You Will Meet a Tall Dark Stranger, Stage Beauty, Bright Young Things.

RADIO INCLUDES: Ethan Frome, The Jinx Element, Mrs Dalloway, Art & Gadg, An American Rose, Restless, Flaw in the Motor/Dust in the Blood, Millions Like Us, Salome, The Golden Notebook, The Porlock Poisoner, Dinner at the Homesick Restaurant, Before They Were Famous, Poetry Please.

THE ENGLISH STAGE COMPANY
AT THE ROYAL COURT THEATRE

'For me the theatre is really a religion or way of life. You must decide what you feel the world is about and what you want to say about it, so that everything in the theatre you work in is saying the same thing ... A theatre must have a recognisable attitude. It will have one, whether you like it or not.'

George Devine, first artistic director of the English Stage Company: notes for an unwritten book.

photo: Stephen Cummiskey

As Britain's leading national company dedicated to new work, the Royal Court Theatre produces new plays of the highest quality, working with writers from all backgrounds, and addressing the problems and possibilities of our time.

"The Royal Court has been at the centre of British cultural life for the past 50 years, an engine room for new writing and constantly transforming the theatrical culture." Stephen Daldry

Since its foundation in 1956, the Royal Court has presented premieres by almost every leading contemporary British playwright, from John Osborne's Look Back in Anger to Caryl Churchill's A Number and Tom Stoppard's Rock 'n' Roll. Just some of the other writers to have chosen the Royal Court to premiere their work include Edward Albee, John Arden, Richard Bean, Samuel Beckett, Edward Bond, Leo Butler, Jez Butterworth, Martin Crimp, Ariel Dorfman, Stella Feehily, Christopher Hampton, David Hare, Eugène Ionesco, Ann Jellicoe, Terry Johnson, Sarah Kane, David Mamet, Martin McDonagh, Conor McPherson, Joe Penhall, Lucy Prebble, Mark Ravenhill, Simon Stephens, Wole Soyinka, Polly Stenham, David Storey, Debbie Tucker Green, Arnold Wesker and Roy Williams.

"It is risky to miss a production there." Financial Times

In addition to its full-scale productions, the Royal Court also facilitates international work at a grass roots level, developing exchanges which bring young writers to Britain and sending British writers, actors and directors to work with artists around the world. The research and play development arm of the Royal Court Theatre, The Studio, finds the most exciting and diverse range of new voices in the UK. The Studio runs play-writing groups including the Young Writers Programme, Critical Mass for black, Asian and minority ethnic writers and the biennial Young Writers Festival. For further information, go to www.royalcourttheatre.com/playwriting/the-studio.

ROYAL COURT SUPPORTERS

The Royal Court has significant and longstanding relationships with many organisations and individuals who provide vital support. It is this support that makes possible its unique playwriting and audience development programmes.

Open Court & Theatre Local are supported by Bloomberg. The Genesis Foundation supports the Royal Court's work with International Playwrights. The Jerwood Charitable Foundation supports emerging writers through the Jerwood New Playwrights programme. The Andrew Lloyd Webber Foundation supports the Royal Court's Studio, which aims to seek out, nurture and support emerging playwrights.

The Harold Pinter Playwright's Award is given annually by his widow, Lady Antonia Fraser, to support a new commission at the Royal Court.

Theatre Local and Open Court supported by

Bloomberg

Supported by
ARTS COUNCIL ENGLAND

Circle Mirror Transformation

Annie Baker's full-length plays include *The Flick*
(Playwrights Horizons; winner of the Susan Smith
Blackburn Award and an Obie Award for Excellence in
Playwriting, Drama Desk and Lucille Lortel nominations
for Best Play), *Circle Mirror Transformation* (Playwrights
Horizons; Obie Award for Best New American Play,
Drama Desk nomination for Best Play), *The Aliens*
(Rattlestick Playwrights Theater and the Bush; Obie
Award for Best New American Play), *Body Awareness*
(Atlantic Theater Company; Drama Desk and Outer
Critics Circle nominations for Best Play/Emerging
Playwright), and an adaptation of Anton Chekhov's
Uncle Vanya, for which she also designed the costumes
(Soho Rep; Drama Desk nomination for Best Revival).
Her plays have been produced throughout the USA at
South Coast Rep, the Guthrie, Victory Gardens, Artists
Rep, Huntington Theater Company, Seattle Rep, Studio
Theatre in DC, Hyde Park Theatre, Kansas City Rep,
Marin Theater Company, A Red Orchid, and over a
hundred other regional theatres. Her work has also been
produced in England, Australia, Argentina, Bolivia,
Chile, Peru, Venezuela, Mexico, Latvia, Sweden and
Russia. She is a Residency Five playwright at the
Signature Theater and a member of New Dramatists,
MCC's Playwrights Coalition and EST. A published
anthology of her work, *The Vermont Plays*, is available
from TCG books.

also by Annie Baker from Faber

THE ALIENS

ANNIE BAKER

Circle Mirror Transformation

ff

faber and faber

Published in 2013 by Faber and Faber Limited
74–77 Great Russell Street, London WC1B 3DA

Circle Mirror Transformation was first published in *The Vermont Plays*
by Annie Baker, Theatre Communications Group, Inc., New York.
Reprinted by permission of the publisher

Typeset by Country Setting, Kingsdown, Kent CT14 8ES
Printed in England by CPI Group (UK) Ltd, Croydon CR0 4YY

A CIP record for this book is available from the British Library

978-0-571-30961-0

MIX
Paper from
responsible sources
FSC® C013604

Circle Mirror Transformation was first performed in the UK at the Rose Lipman Building, Haggerston, London, on 5 July 2013, presented by the Royal Court Theatre as part of the Theatre Local season. The cast was as follows:

Marty Imelda Staunton
James Danny Webb
Schultz Toby Jones
Theresa Fenella Woolgar
Lauren Shannon Tarbet

Director James Macdonald
Designer Chloe Lamford
Lighting Designer Peter Mumford
Sound Designer Carolyn Downing

Playwrights Horizons, Inc., New York City, produced the world premiere of *Circle Mirror Transformation* off-Broadway in 2009. The play was developed, in part, with the assistance of the Sundance Institute Theatre Program, with additional support from the Sundance Institute's Time Warner Storytelling Fellowship.

Characters

Marty
fifty-five

James
sixty

Schultz
forty-eight

Theresa
thirty-five

Lauren
sixteen

Setting

A windowless dance studio in the town
of Shirley, Vermont. There is a wall of mirrors.
There is a big blue yoga ball. Summertime.

Note

The week titles (WEEK ONE, WEEK TWO, etc.)
should somehow be projected and / or displayed
onstage.

A slash (/) indicates overlapping dialogue.

Author's Note

*To anyone interested in putting on
a production of this play*

Please heed the pauses and the silences. They are of great importance – they are just as important as the dialogue – and every one of them was placed in the script with extreme care. If you skip over or rush through these silences, you are performing a different play.

There will be a point in the rehearsal process where it seems like these pauses and silences are slowing the play down. The actors will worry that the play is boring – that they'll lose the audience's attention – that what they need to do is *pick up the pace.*

All I can say is, this is an inevitable feeling and you must fight against it.

Without its silences, this play is a satire, and with its silences it is, hopefully, a strange little meditation on theatre and life and death and the passing of time.

Pauses should last at least two full seconds or more, long pauses four full seconds or more, and the silences should feel potentially endless.

I hope that you will portray these characters with compassion. They are not fools. And if you ask me, I think Marty's a great teacher.

CIRCLE MIRROR TRANSFORMATION

Prologue

Lights up. Marty, James, Theresa, Lauren and Schultz are all lying on the floor, in various positions.
    After at least fifteen seconds of silence:

Theresa One.

   A long silence.

James Two.

   Silence.

Lauren / Schultz Three.

Marty Start again.

   Silence.

Schultz One.

Marty Two.

James Three.

   Another long silence.

Lauren Four.

Marty . . . Five.

James Six.

   Silence.

Theresa / Schultz Seven.

Schultz Shoot.

Marty Start again.

   Silence.

Schultz / James One.

Lauren . . . Oh my God.

Marty Okay. Wait.
  We're not getting it.

  Pause.

Let's all . . . everyone take a deep breath.

  Pause.

Okay.

  About five seconds go by.

James One.

  Silence.

Theresa / Lauren Two.

Marty Start again.

  Blackout.

Week One

James is standing centre stage, facing the audience. The rest of the class sits downstage, facing James.

James Hi. My name is Marty Kreisberg. Short for Martha, but they've been calling me Marty since I was born.
Ah . . .

He scratches his head, then grins.

My husband is supposed to do this, ah, monologue about me but he doesn't really know what to –

Marty is trying to signal something to him.

Why can't I do that?

He shakes his head.

Allrightallright.
I'm fifty-five and I'm, ah . . . I live in Shirley, Vermont. I'm co-executive director here at the Community Center and I also teach a bunch of classes . . . ah . . . Pottery, Jewellery-Making, Creative Drama for Youth . . . I've been pushing for an adult Creative Drama class for a while and I'm . . . I'm really glad they let me do it.

Pause.

Okay.
Ah . . . I'm from New Jersey. Originally. I don't have any kids, but I'm a great stepmother. My husband is named James. He's in the class too.
Ah . . . let's see. I'm really into non-traditional healing and sort of . . . unconventional, ah . . .

He scratches his head again.

I'm fifty-five years old. I really love the Southwest. I hope
to move there some day.
   Did I already say that?
   Okay.

Blackout.

TWO

*Theresa, Schultz, Lauren and James are all walking
around the room in different directions, sock-footed. This
should last at least thirty seconds. Everyone is taking this
seriously. Marty is sitting on her yoga ball, watching.*

Marty . . . Faster.

*They all walk a little faster, still going in different
directions.*

. . . Even faster.

*They start zooming around the room, except for
Lauren, who tries to keep a safe distance away from
everyone.*

Now . . . I want you to slow down.

Pause.

Start noticing everyone around you.

*They all keep walking while making an effort to notice
everyone around them. About twenty seconds pass.*

. . . And I want you to find people and shake their hand.

They obey. About twenty more seconds pass.

Now say your name when you shake hands!

About thirty seconds of walking/shaking hands/saying your own name.

Okay! Good. Great. Stop.

They stop and look at her. She smiles at them.

How'd that feel?

An awkward silence.

Theresa	**Schultz**
Great.	Weird.
	. . . Good.

Marty Okay.

She gets up off her ball.

Um.
Well.
Welcome,

Pause.

I just . . . I'm so excited to get to know all of you.

An even longer pause.

I um . . . I don't want to talk too much, because that's . . .

She makes a vague gesture with her hands.

But. Um. I just hope that you all feel, um, safe here. And open.
And willing to *go* with it.
Ah . . . okay.
Let's keep going!

Blackout.

THREE

Marty, Theresa, Lauren, James and Schultz are sitting in a circle.

Marty I

Theresa Took

Lauren This

James Class

Schultz Because

Marty It

Theresa Was

Lauren In

James The

Schultz . . . Paper.

A weird pause.

Marty Love

Theresa . . . Truth!

Lauren Um . . . discovery

James Self-Actualisation

Schultz . . . Friends

Marty Were

Theresa Part

Lauren Of

James All

Schultz The

Marty Mess!

Theresa And

Lauren Stuff.

Pause.

James . . . Enormous.

A confused pause.

Schultz I

Marty Feel

Theresa Fantastic!

Lauren Period.

Marty Oh. Hey. Yeah. I forgot to – we don't have to . . . you don't have to say 'period'. You can just / keep –

James Pain

Schultz Um . . . ah . . . Loneliness

Marty Are

Theresa Feeding

Lauren Me

James . . . Sky.

Pause.

Schultz Evil

Marty . . . Blue

Theresa Birds

Lauren Fly

James Over

Schultz Head.

Pause.

Marty Green

Theresa Wondrous

Lauren Um . . . sunshine

James Washes

Schultz Over

Marty My

Theresa Little

Lauren Tiny

James Face

Pause.

Schultz . . . Hopefully.

Pause.

Marty Okay.
Great.

Pause.

Maybe next week we'll try to make it a little more like a real story.

Blackout.

FOUR

Breaktime.
Schultz and Theresa are the only people in the room. Theresa is squatting in the corner, listening to a cell phone message. Schultz is drinking from a bottle of water and eyeing her.

Schultz How long did she say?

Theresa holds up one finger and mouths 'Sorry'. After a few seconds she snaps her phone shut.

Theresa Sorry. What?

Schultz How long did she . . .

A pause while he tries to reformulate his thoughts.

Ah . . .
How long is the break?

Theresa I think she said ten minutes?

Schultz nods, embarrassed, and goes back to drinking water. Theresa watches him drink and smiles at him. He puts down the water and smiles back at her.

Schultz I'm sorry. You have . . .
Sorry. Do you / ah –

Theresa What?

Schultz I just ah . . .
I was going to say that you have very . . . you have very alive *eyes*.

Theresa Oh. Wow. I –

Schultz But that sounds / kind of –

Theresa No! Thank you.

Schultz I don't mean it in a, uh . . . in a weird way.

Theresa No. It's a – it's a compliment.

They smile at each other. A pause.

Schultz What's your deal?

Theresa Oh. God. I / um –

Schultz I just mean . . . I haven't seen you around. It's a small town, / so –

Theresa I moved here like five months ago.

Schultz All right.

A pause.

Theresa Do you live near here? Or do / you –

Schultz I live in the Brook.

Theresa I'm . . . what? Sorry. / The –

Schultz They're condos. The Brook. It's on Hitchcock? Right off Seven. Across from / the –

Theresa Oh yeah. I know where that is.

A silence, during which Theresa notices his wedding ring.

So do you live there alone or do / you –

Schultz I live there alone.

Pause.

My wife and I recently . . . we're divorced. That's why I live in the, uh . . . I moved out about a year ago.

Theresa Oh. Okay.

Schultz She lives in our house. It's a great house. With a . . . I spent years working on the garden.

Theresa Huh.

Schultz The Brook is . . . it's very corporate. Very corporate-feeling.

Theresa smiles sympathetically at him. Another silence.

Theresa I was just confused because you, um . . . you're still wearing your wedding ring.

Schultz looks down at his hand.

Schultz Yes. Yes I am.

Lauren enters, her cell phone pressed to her ear. She eyes them suspiciously, then goes over to her bag, rummages through it, removes something, slips it into her pocket, and then leaves. They watch her.

I should probably take it off.

Theresa Yeah. I don't know. What's the rush, I guess.

Pause.

Schultz Would you be interested / in –

Marty and James enter, in the middle of talking.

James So *she* called *you*.

Marty Yeah. We / just –

James What'd you talk about?

Marty Nothing really.

She looks up and smiles at Theresa and James.

We've got about three more minutes, you guys.

James walks out of the room and heads to the bathroom. A weird silence. Marty's cell phone rings. She takes it out and looks at it, then puts it back in her pocket.

Schultz (*to Theresa*) So you're a . . . you like to hula-hoop!

Theresa Um. The correct term is actually hooping.

Schultz Oh God. I'm sorry.

Theresa No, no. It's a common, um . . . but 'hula-hooping' is, actually, um . . . it's a misnaming.

Schultz Ah.

Schultz keeps staring at the hoop. James re-enters and stands near the doorway, watching Schultz and Theresa.

Schultz It's big.

Theresa The big ones are actually easier to use. Wanna see?

Marty We're about to start. Whenever Lauren gets back.

Theresa It'll take two seconds.

Theresa runs over to the corner, gets the hoop, and runs back to the centre of the room. Schultz stands aside while she raises the hoop to her hips and then, with a few small, deft tilts of her pelvis, begins hooping.

Schultz . . . Wow.

Theresa continues hooping. After a while:

Theresa The key is actually less movement.

Schultz Uh-huh.

Theresa As opposed to more movement.

Now Marty and James are watching, too. Everyone is a little hypnotised.

Schultz Jesus.

Theresa stops and gracefully catches the hoop before it falls to the ground.

Theresa (*to Schultz*) Try it.

Schultz Oh. No. I can't. / I ah –

Theresa It's actually really easy.

Schultz shakes his head.

Schultz.

Schultz Nope.

Lauren re-enters, turning off her cell phone.

Marty Oop! You know what? Everyone's back. Let's get /
started.

James (*suddenly*) I'll try it.

Theresa Yeah James!

*James walks over to Theresa. She hands him the hoop,
and he steps into it.*

James What do I do?

Theresa Okay. Just um . . . put one foot forward.

James puts one foot forward.

James Uh-huh.

Theresa Now just . . . try it. Don't think too much.

*James throws his pelvis forward and sends the hoop
aloft. It crashes to the ground in about three seconds.*

James (*shaking his head*) Ah.

Theresa Try again. It's just a little motion. Like a little . . .
spin.

*James tries again. He sends the hoop aloft, awkwardly
swinging his hips back and forth.*

Good! Oh my God! That's awesome!

*Everyone watches James, half impressed, half aghast.
The hoop crashes to the ground. Schultz and Theresa
and Lauren all applaud. James hands the hoop back
to Theresa.*

Marty That was amazing.

Blackout.

Lights up. They are all sitting in a circle. Marty is in the middle of a story. Everyone is rapt.

Marty And it was at this . . . this wedding was like . . . it was a real hippie wedding. We were all sleeping on the floor of . . . we were sleeping in the lobby of this old abandoned hotel in Eureka. And I spread out my little straw mat – this was at the end of the night, and we were all a little drunk, and we'd been dancing, and singing, and I was about to go to sleep, but then I looked over . . . and next to me, lying on his little straw mat, was this, um, this *guy*.

   Pause.

This really cute guy. I'd seen him earlier that night dancing with all . . . I mean, he was constantly surrounded by women.
   And I hadn't gotten a chance to talk to him, but I'd noticed him.

   Pause.

So we were all lying in the dark, so I couldn't quite tell if . . . but then my eyes started adjusting and I said: holy . . . this guy lying next to me is . . . this adorable guy is just staring at me and smiling at me.
   And we just lay there smiling at each other for the next couple of hours.
   Not touching or . . .
   I don't even remember when we fell asleep. And the next morning we woke up, smiled at each other again, and he said: I'm James.

Schultz (*softly*) I knew it.

Marty And I said: I'm Marty.

And he said . . . I couldn't believe the . . . without any kind of . . . he just said, with total . . . 'Wannago camping with me tomorrow? I'm driving north to Arcata.'

I couldn't believe the nerve of this guy! And I had all these obligations back in . . .

But I found myself saying . . . I just said:

'Sure. Why not.'

James grins, embarrassed. Schultz applauds a little. A long pause.

Theresa That is really really cute.

Another pause.

Marty Okay. Who else has a story? And don't forget to really listen, you guys. We're gonna have to remember these.

Pause.

Theresa I'll go.

Marty Perfect.

Theresa stands up, somewhat unnecessarily.

Theresa Okay. Well. This one time when I was still living in New York? I was on the . . . there was this old Jewish guy in my subway car. I knew he was Jewish because . . . well, he was stereotypically Jewish. I mean, not that all Jews look this way, obviously, but he had this humungous nose and this long like white beard with these big glasses and he had this accent like an old Jewish Yiddishy Brooklyn accent and these . . . um . . . suspenders kind of pants.

Anyway.

The point is he was very clearly Jewish and he was sitting there talking to these old black guys. Who seemed kind of crazy. They all seemed crazy. But he was holding these pamphlets and he was yelling at them, not angry just kind of yelling all this stuff and they were nodding and saying like 'Totally, man' or like 'You're so right,' and I started listening and he was talking about this Jewish Conspiracy and he used the phrase 'Jew S.A.' And then he was like: 'Do you think the World Trade Towers came down by themselves?' And then he was talking about how, you know, the Jews killed Christ, and then . . . ah . . . what else? Oh. Something about World War Two. How that happened because Jews were running Wall Street and Wall Street paid for Germany or something?

A very long, weird silence. No one knows what to do.

I guess that's it.

She sits down.

Marty What made you think of that story?

Theresa Um. I don't know. I think about it when . . . you know. The issue of self-hate or whatever.

Silence.

Marty That man may not have been Jewish.

Theresa Oh. Um. I'm pretty sure he was.

Marty He may have fit your stereo . . . He may have fit your stereotype of a Jewish person but he may not have been Jewish.

Another silence. Finally Marty looks at her watch.

Okay. It looks like we're out of time!

Everyone starts getting up.

Thanks, you guys.
I think this was a really really great start.

They all start going over to the corner to get their bags, put on their shoes, turn on their cell phones, etc.

Hey – Lauren? I almost forgot. Just before you – I think you still owe me a cheque?

Lauren My mom was supposed to mail it to you.

Marty I don't think I . . . Would you be willing to remind her?

Lauren Um. Yeah. Sure.

Blackout.

Week Two

Lauren is standing centre stage, facing the audience.
Everyone else sits downstage, facing Lauren.

Lauren Hi.

My name is Schultz.

I'm a carpenter.

And I don't just . . . I mean, I do regular carpenter
things but I also make these amazing chairs that are like
. . . this one chair has, like . . . like the head-rest is the
sun and the whole thing is gold?

Lauren looks nervously at Schultz.

It's kind of hard to explain.

There's this other chair that looks like a cloud.

Um . . . I'm forty-eight years old.

I grew up in Maryland and my mom died when I was
really little. She was an elementary school teacher. I
always wanted to be a baseball player.

Um . . .

I'm really nice to everyone.

Pause.

I met my wife Becky right out of college and we . . .

Schultz is trying to subtly indicate something to her.

Yeah. I know. I was gonna –

We just separated. Divorced.

I'm in a lot of pain about it.

But, um, to look on the bright side, I have more time
now to work on my chairs and maybe find a way for
them to um, spread out to um, more people.

Pause.

I am an artist.
   I am a really good artist.

Blackout.

TWO

Schultz, James, Theresa and Lauren are playing a particularly confusing and chaotic version of Explosion Tag while Marty stands in the corner and watches. Explosion Tag is basically regular tag except you're supposed to 'explode' when tagged. When you're tagged you also become 'It', and as 'It' you're supposed to be exploding constantly. When the lights come up Lauren is 'It'. Everyone is awkwardly darting around the room. Lauren is exploding vocally, not physically (she keeps saying 'powccchrrrpowpow'), and half-heartedly scurrying after people. Everyone has a different way of eluding her, although it is not very difficult. This can last up to a minute. Finally Lauren tags Schultz on the elbow. It is unclear whether or not he purposely let this happen.

Lauren You're It.

Schultz makes a melodic falling-bomb sound ('NEEEEEEeeeeeerrrr'), while sinking to his knees. There is a long pause while he remains there, still. Everyone stops and watches. Finally Schultz explodes: silently, beautifully, atomically. His arms are thrust out, his eyes are wide open, his mouth is gaping open in a silent scream.

Marty . . . Gorgeous.

Schultz falls backwards on to the floor and lies on his back. There is a long silence while everyone remains standing, watching him.

Marty You're It now, Schultz.

Schultz (*sitting up*) Oh. Sorry.

Schultz reaches out, quick as a snake, and grabs James's ankle.

James Ah! Jesus.

Schultz You're It.

Blackout.

THREE

Breaktime.
Marty and Theresa are squatting by their bags in the corner, talking quietly. Schultz is lurking in the other corner, drinking from his water bottle.

Theresa It's natural.

Marty It *is?*

Theresa Weird, right?

Marty Well. It's beautiful.

Theresa Thanks.

Marty Have you . . .

A pause.

I just . . . I saw them in CVS the other day, and I . . . Have you seen these things?

Theresa Wait, what are you talking about?

Marty These, um . . . they're like these little packets of dye, but they're . . .

She giggles, then whispers.

. . . They're for . . . it's for pubic hair.

Theresa Oh my God.

Marty They were in their own little section, and I was, I said: Oh. My. God. And I called James over and he said: what's the big deal?

Theresa Well. Of / course. He –

Marty And I was in a huff about it, I was in this big huff, and then I thought . . .

Marty stops talking and glances over at Schultz.

Theresa (*giggling*) Can you hear us, Schultz?

Schultz lowers his water bottle.

Schultz What? No.

Marty and Theresa dissolve into more giggles. Schultz looks tormented.

I have to check my, uh . . . my phone messages.

Schultz takes his cell phone out of his pocket, crosses to the front corner of the room, and pretends (convincingly) to listen to a message.

Theresa So you were really angry –

Marty I was in a big huff about it, but then I . . . Oh God. You probably don't have to worry about this. You're too young. But my, um . . . that hair is half *grey* now and it drives me crazy . . . and I / thought –

Theresa Did you buy it?

Marty I'm thinking about it.

Theresa Oh my God. Awesome.

Marty But then James will . . . I know he's going to accuse me of being a hypocrite.

Theresa I bet he'll like it.

Marty Theresa.

Theresa I bet he will.

Marty shakes her head.

Marty I have to pee.

Marty gets up and exits. Silence. Schultz is still listening to the imaginary message. Theresa smiles at him.

Theresa Hey.

Schultz snaps his phone shut.

Schultz Hi.

Theresa How was your week?

Schultz It was okay.

Pause.

How was your week?

Theresa It was good.

Pause.

I bought a plant!

Schultz Oh yeah? What kind?

Theresa Um . . . I don't know. The tag says that it's a 'money plant'? Like if you put it under – if you put it in the window you'll make a lot of money or something.

Schultz Wow.

Silence.

Theresa Who called you?

Schultz My friend.

Theresa Oh.

Another silence. Theresa looks at the door, then back at Schultz.

So what do you think?

Schultz I ah . . .?

Theresa About the class.

Schultz Huh. Well . . .

He glances nervously towards the door.

Uh . . . I like it. I don't feel . . . I guess I'm having a little trouble feeling totally comfortable?

Theresa Yeah.

Schultz I feel pretty self-conscious.

Theresa You'll get the hang of it.

Schultz You seem so . . . you're so good at everything.

Theresa Well. I'm / actually –

Schultz You do everything in such a . . . You're so graceful.

Theresa Oh God. That's . . .

She shakes her head and grins. They look at each other. A long silence.

Schultz.

Schultz What.

Theresa Do you maybe wanna get a cup of coffee after class? Or um . . .

Schultz stands there, speechless. Theresa is confused. After a pause:

I'm sorry. Did I do something wrong?

Schultz No.
   I mean yes.
   Didn't I say yes?

Theresa You didn't say anything.

Schultz Oh God. Yes.
   I'm sorry. I thought I said yes.
   Yes!

   Blackout.

FOUR

James, Schultz, Theresa and Lauren are sitting up against the stage-right wall. Marty is in the centre of the room, facing them.

Marty Okay. So I'm going to use myself as an example.

   They all nod. Marty taps her chin thoughtfully.

Schultz.

Schultz Yes.

Marty Will you be my father?

Schultz Gladly.

   He stands up. She takes hold of his arm and leads him into the centre of the room.

Marty (*to the group*) Don't be afraid to physically take hold of people and guide them. That's the point. Okay.

   Pause.

(*To Schultz.*) All right. Um . . . let's see. You are . . .
You're . . . You're a very condescending . . .
   You're always kind of quietly Looking Down on everyone. So maybe . . .

Marty manipulates Schultz's arms until they're folded across his chest. Schultz is thoroughly enjoying himself.

And also . . . you have this certain . . .

She reaches up and pushes his eyebrows.

You have a condescending sort of . . .

Schultz raises his eyebrows in exaggerated contempt.

Perfect.
Okay. Stay that way.

She turns back to the group.

Now. Theresa. I want you to be my mother.

Theresa Awesome.

Theresa leaps up. Marty guides her towards the centre of the room and puts her next to Schultz.

Marty Okay. You are . . . you're very angry. You're this very aggressive, very dominating woman . . . People have always asked so much of you and not respected your intelligence and so you're really . . .

Marty manipulates Theresa's hands so that she's clutching her own hair.

And if you could turn toward Schultz . . . your husband . . .

Theresa turns towards Schultz.

And . . .

Marty takes hold of Theresa's mouth. This surprises Theresa a little.

And just . . . you're screaming at him.
Good. Good.
And Lauren?

Lauren (*not getting up*) Yeah.

Marty You're me.

A pause.

Can you get up?

Lauren gets up. This time Marty doesn't go over and take her arm. Instead Lauren slowly walks towards the rear of the room.

I want you to sit on the ground.

Lauren sits cross-legged on the ground.

Except I want you to hug your knees.

Lauren obeys.

Yep. And kind of bury your head in . . .
Yep.

Marty observes for a while.

That looks great.

She looks over at James, who is still seated against the wall.

Don't they look great?

He nods. Silence.

Wow.
Okay. You can relax.

Theresa and Schultz exhale and let their arms drop to their sides, laughing. Lauren lifts her head up a little but doesn't move otherwise.

Schultz Can I go next?

Marty Of course! Yes. Everyone back at the wall.

Everyone starts heading back to the wall.

And this is just the beginning! Next week we start re-enactments.

Blackout.

FIVE

They are all lying on the floor again. The lights are dimmed.

Schultz One.

Marty Two.

Theresa Three.

Long silence.

Theresa Four.

Silence.

Schultz FIVE.

Silence.

James Six.

Silence.

Schultz / Lauren Seven.

Marty Start again.

Silence.
Blackout.

Week Three

Schultz, centre stage, is facing the audience. Everyone else sits downstage, facing Schultz.

Schultz My name is Theresa.
Ah . . . I am a very special person.

He looks tenderly in Theresa's direction.

I am thirty-five years old.
I'm very passionate. About all things. I care about things very deeply.

Pause.

I grew up in a small town in New Hampshire. I have a younger brother named Brendan. He's getting married next summer.
Ah . . . I lived in New York for about . . . for many years. I was . . . I am an actress. The decision to move to Vermont was a difficult but I think ultimately positive one. There was a competitiveness and a claustrophobia that was very difficult for me in New York . . . also this sense that people didn't really care about each other.

He shoots another tender look at Theresa.

I have always wanted to make a difference. I have an amazing soul, an amazing warmth, that, that, that people can sense the minute they meet me. I had hoped to reach people through theatre, but the realisation that maybe this was impossible caused me to re-evaluate and try living in a, a smaller place, where I could work, uh, directly with people. I'm studying for a certificate in acupressure and, ah . . .

Shoot.
Rolfing.
Rolfing.

About six months before I left New York I broke up with my boyfriend, Mark. He was not very good to me. Sometimes I guilt myself out and convince myself that I ruined something and that I made a mistake, but those, uh, my friends and people who are close to me know that I did the right thing. That was a toxic relationship.

My father has prostate cancer. It's a, ah, blessing to be only a few hours away from him and to be able to see him on the weekends. I'm also worried about my mother.

I don't want my parents to die.

A long pause while he thinks deeply about this.

Yeah. Okay. That's it.

Blackout.

TWO

Theresa, James and Lauren are standing against the wall. Schultz is standing in the centre of the room, whispering to Marty. She nods, smiling.

Marty . . . Okay.
Yeah.
Yes. Beautiful.

He thinks, then whispers something again.

Sure.

She turns and smiles at Theresa, James and Lauren.

We're just figuring this out.

Schultz whispers something to her again.

Well. Either way.

Schultz nods. Marty walks back to the wall and stands against it with Lauren, Theresa and James. A long silence while Schultz stands there, looking around the room, troubled.

Why don't you start with your bed?

Schultz (*to James*) Will you be my bed?

James Ah . . .

He looks at Marty.

Sure.

James steps forward.

Marty What did your bed look like?

Schultz . . . It was small.

Pause.

It was next to my window.

Marty Can you describe some of the . . . some of its special qualities to James?

A silence.

Schultz Small.

Pause.

Soft.

Marty looks at James. Slowly, a little creakily, James gets on his hands and knees. They all watch him.

Marty Great. What's next?

Schultz Ah –

Marty What's something you loved about your childhood bedroom?

Schultz . . . The tree outside my window.

Marty Perfect.

Schultz (*to Theresa*) Will you be the tree?

Theresa Of course.

Theresa steps forward.

What kind of tree?

Schultz Ah . . . maple.

Theresa Am I large or small?

Schultz Large.

Theresa stands near James and strikes a beautiful tree pose.

Oh. Yeah.

Schultz and Theresa smile at each other.

(*To Lauren*.) Ah . . . will you be my baseball glove?

Lauren Um . . .

Marty What are some of the qualities of your baseball glove that you'd like Lauren to embody?

Schultz Uh . . .

Lauren plops down on the ground, cross-legged.

Yeah. Okay.

Marty What else, Schultz? What else did you love about your bedroom?

Schultz Ah . . .

Pause.

My stuffed snake.

Marty Your –

Schultz Right before she died my mother, uh . . . she gave me this stuffed animal. A, ah . . . a stuffed snake.

Silence.

Marty Do you want me / to –

Schultz Yeah.

Marty Where do you want me to go?

Schultz Will you sit on my bed?

Marty nods. She sits on James's back and mimes, as best she can, the position of a stuffed snake.

Marty (*still in stuffed-snake position*) Okay. Now . . . take a step back . . . and look at your bedroom.

Schultz takes a step back. They all freeze in their positions. He looks at them for a while.

What are you feeling?

Schultz Ah . . .

Pause.

It doesn't really . . .
  I'm sorry.

Pause,

I ah . . .
  It doesn't really look like my bedroom.

Marty Does it feel like your bedroom?

Schultz shakes his head. A sad silence.

. . . Well. Okay.

Schultz Sorry.

Marty No. No. It's fine.

She gets off James's back, a little embarrassed.

Let's um . . . We can all . . . Everybody can relax.

James and Lauren get up immediately. Schultz smiles at Theresa.

Schultz You were great.

Blackout.

THREE

Breaktime.
Theresa is by herself, sitting by her bag, listening to her messages. Schultz enters. He walks over to her, touches her hair, then kneels down and tries to kiss her.

Theresa Hold on. I have to finish listening to my –

Schultz keeps trying to kiss her.

Schultz. Hold on a second.

Schultz stops and waits. After a second she snaps her phone shut. They look at each other. After a second, he leans in again and they kiss. She stops and looks nervously around the room.

Schultz They're out feeding the meter.

Theresa What about Lauren?

Schultz (*softly*) I thought about you this morning. In the shower.

They begin to kiss again. After a few seconds Lauren walks in, sees them, freezes, and walks out. They do not see her. After more kissing:

45

Theresa ... Oh God.
Okay.
We have to stop.

Schultz looks at his watch.

Schultz We have three more minutes.

Theresa Schultz.

Schultz Come into the bathroom with me.

Theresa I think that's probably a bad / id—

Schultz Just for a minute. Just for a minute.

*He starts walking out the door. A little reluctantly,
Theresa follows. The room is empty for twenty-five
seconds. Then Lauren re-enters, looking a little
traumatised. She puts her bag down. She isn't sure
what to do. She stands facing the mirrors, looking at
herself. She frowns, then walks closer and inspects a
pimple on her chin. After a little while Marty enters,
looking at her phone. She sees Lauren and smiles.*

Marty Hey, Lauren.

Lauren ... Hey.

Marty Are you excited about school starting in a few
weeks?

Lauren Um.
I'm not sure.

Marty laughs a little.

Marty That's understandable. I guess school is a mixed
bag.

*A long pause while Marty smiles at Lauren. Then
Marty walks over to her bag in the corner and starts
rummaging through it.*

Lauren (*suddenly*) Hey.
Um.
I have a question.

Marty (*looking up*) Yes.

Lauren Um . . .

A long silence.

Are we going to be doing any real acting?

Another silence.

Marty . . . What do you mean by 'real acting'?

Lauren Um . . .

Pause.

Like acting out a play. Or something. I don't know.

Pause.

Like reading from a . . .

She trails off.

Marty Um. Well. Honestly? I don't think so.

Another silence.

Lauren Okay.

Marty Did you . . . were you looking forward to that?

Lauren Um . . . I signed up for this class because I thought we were gonna act.

Marty We are acting.

Lauren . . . Yeah.

Pause. She sighs.

Okay. Thanks.

Lauren exits. Marty watches her go. After a few seconds James enters.

James She won't pick up. Her ~~phone~~ is on. She just won't pick up.

Marty Do you want me to call her?

James No. That's absurd.

Pause.

She's so fucking ungrateful.

Marty I don't know if I agree with that assessment.

James Okay. Could you please –

Schultz and Theresa enter, holding hands. Theresa drops Schultz's hand the second she sees other people in the room, then goes over to her bag and starts looking through it. Schultz is smiling. James looks at Schultz.

What?

Schultz Sorry?

James You're smiling like something . . . like something hilarious just happened.

Schultz Oh. Ah . . . no. Sorry.

Blackout.

FOUR

James and Theresa, standing, are facing each other. Schultz and Lauren and Marty watch.

James (*hello*) Ak mak.

Theresa (*hello*) Goulash.

48

James Ak mak?

Theresa Ah . . . goulash. Goulash.

James Ak. Mak.

James giggles.

Marty Stay in it.

Theresa (*becoming serious – 'I have something to tell you'*) Goulash . . . goulash goulash goulash.

James (*what is it?*) Ak mak.

Theresa (*sometimes, at night, I feel incredibly lonely*) Goulash, goulash, goulash goulash goulash.

James (*I don't understand what you're saying*) Ak mak, ak mak.

Theresa (*I lie in bed staring at the ceiling, and I think about couples and families, like you and Marty*) Goulash goulash goulash goulash, goulash goulash goulash goulash, goulash goulash goulash goulash.

James (*you are very beautiful*) Ak mak, ak mak ak mak ak mak.

Theresa (*are you sad too?*) Goulash?

James (*I am attracted to you*) Ak mak.

Theresa (*you're sad, too, I knew it*) Goulash goulash goulash. Goulash.

James (*I feel really guilty when I think about how attracted I am to you*) Ak mak ak mak ak mak ak mak.

A long silence.

Theresa (*I feel like you understand me*) Goulash goulash.

James (*I feel like you actually understand me*) Ak mak ak mak.

They gaze at each other.

Marty Okay. Good. Stop. What were they communicating?

Schultz . . . They seemed very connected.

Marty Uh-huh. Good.

Lauren They were in love.

A silence.

It seemed like they were in love.

Another silence.

Marty Huh.
Okay.
Um . . . what was actually happening, though? What was being sad? Sorry. Said. What was being said?

Silence.

Schultz Uh . . . well . . . I mean, the sentiment / was –

Lauren At first she seemed upset.

Schultz It seemed like she was sharing a secret.

Lauren Yeah. Like a . . .

Schultz But I thought that . . . it felt like James understood her.

Theresa (*softly*) I'm sorry. Excuse me.

She quickly walks out of the room and shuts the door. Silence.

James Should / someone –

Schultz I will.

Marty No. That's okay. I'll be right back.

She walks out of the room and shuts the door. Blackout.

The group stands in a circle. Theresa starts swinging her arms back and forth and making a corresponding sound.

Theresa WOOP. WOOP. WOOP. WOOP.

Marty Let's all mirror it back to her!

Everyone mirrors the gesture/sound back to Theresa, in unison. After a few seconds of this:

Now Lauren! Transform it!

Lauren, after a second of hesitation, transforms the gesture/sound into a different gesture/sound. The whole group mirrors it back to her. They go round the circle, twice, playing Circle Mirror Transformation. This is the only improvised part of the play. Except: the exercise should end with Schultz transforming someone else's gesture into a form of solemn and silent davening. Everyone silently davens on their knees for a while.
  Blackout.

Week Four

ONE

Schultz enters the room, in darkness. He is the first one there. He switches on the lights. He puts his backpack down, drinks some water, gives himself a long look in the mirror, and then starts doing knee-bends and touching his toes.

Theresa enters, carrying her hula-hoop. She starts a little when she sees Schultz.

Theresa Hey.

Schultz Hey.

A very long, agonising silence.

Theresa I'm sorry I didn't / call you last –

Schultz You don't need to apologise.

Silence.

Theresa I know I don't.

Silence.

But I'm sorry I didn't call you back.

Schultz Twice.

Theresa What?

Schultz You didn't call me back twice.

Theresa . . . I'm sorry.

Schultz shrugs and takes a long drink from his water. Theresa watches him for a while.

You seem angry.

Schultz lowers the water and sighs.

Schultz Um . . . I think I'm . . . I think I'm a little disappointed.
In you.
But. Uh. I'm not *angry*.

A long silence.

Theresa Well. You shouldn't be disappointed in me.

Pause.

Because I've made it . . . I've made it really, really clear that I / can't –

Schultz Yes. Thank you. Okay.

Theresa Schultz.

Schultz It's just . . . it's funny. The not-calling.
Because a week and a half ago you were calling me every day.

Pause.

Theresa Yeah.

Schultz So . . . it's just . . .

Pause.

I'm at a really vulnerable place in my life right / now, and –

Theresa So am I!

Schultz – and the, uh, I really don't need someone who – someone who's going to be inconsistent?

Silence.

Theresa I'm sorry.

Schultz convulses in horrible, strained, silent laughter.

I won't be . . . I won't be inconsistent any more.

I think we . . . I think the best thing might be for . . . maybe we should take a break from seeing each other. Outside of . . . and then I won't have to

The door opens. It's Marty and James and Lauren. They all come in together, with their purses, backpacks, etc. Lauren and Marty are in the middle of a tense exchange.

Lauren She said she mailed it to you three weeks ago.

Marty Okay. Sure. But I never got it.

Lauren Maybe it got lost in the mail.

Marty All right. Fine. But then she has to cancel it and . . .

Marty notices Theresa and Schultz.

Is everything okay?

Theresa (*after a pause*) Mmhm.

Blackout.

TWO

Theresa, centre stage, beaming, is facing the audience. Everyone else sits downstage, facing Theresa.

Theresa I'm James.

I grew up in a lot of different places because my father was in the army. Um . . . Germany. Chicago. Florida. I spent the last, um, three years of high school in Long Beach, California, so that was nice 'cause I got to graduate with people I knew and make real friends.

I went to school at UC Santa Barbara, which was pretty crazy in the late sixties! I learned a lot about myself during college. One, it was pretty hard to break away from my father and all his expectations for me. I also learned a lot about women and men and sexual politics.

Um . . . I have a really funny story about avoiding the draft . . .

She glances briefly at James and grins.

. . . but, um, okay.

I travelled around a lot after college. I lived in Monterey. I lived at this crazy camp ground and I had to um, when I did my laundry I would hang my clothes out on the tree branches. Um . . . I went to law school. That was a really different world. But I got really interested on my own in, um, Marxist philosophy, and, um, oh . . . I met my first wife there. Her name was Sylvia. We got married a couple of years later. Um . . . what else. Oh God.

There's just a lot of good stuff.

I'm really interesting.

She giggles.

Um. Okay. I got through law school and I landed myself this really like great job at a firm in Berkeley and then the day of the bar exam came and I went there and I sat down at the desk and I looked down at the paper in front of me and then I just, like, put down my pencil and I walked out.

Because I realised at that moment that I didn't want to participate in that. In the system. I didn't want to contribute to like a fundamentally flawed . . .

A pause, she glances at Marty.

Oh God. Okay. Sorry. I'll stop um . . .

I have a daughter! Her name is Erin. She's my only child but I wish we were a little closer . . .

Theresa sobers up a little.

. . . and that's hard for me.

She's close with Marty. Marty is my wife.

She grins.

Marty is *awesome*.

We live in this amazing house near the centre of town painted these really amazing colours. It's like purple and orange and yellow and people stop their cars and take pictures of it. We have a cat named Coltrane.

Coltrane only has three legs.

She giggles again.

Um . . . okay.

I am . . .

She sobers up and thinks again.

I am a very strong man. By strong I don't mean physically strong, although, um, that too. I've been through a lot. My first wife was an alcoholic. My whole family is alcoholics. Alcoholic. My father was emotionally abusive to my mother and although I'm not that way I feel a lot of his anger inside of me. I feel it and I think instead of dealing with it I push it, um, I push it deep down inside me and repress it.

A pause.

But the truth is . . . I mean, I haven't said this. But . . .

I think the problem is not my father so much as my fear of being my father. Like if I run away too hard from him I will become something else that is also problematic.

Because actually?

I'm an amazing person.

She grins.

Okay. Thank you.

Blackout.

THREE

Lights up. Theresa, Marty, Schultz and James stand in a line. Lauren is facing them.

Lauren Um.

Silence. Lauren steps forward. She taps James on the shoulder.

You're my dad. Neil. You're Neil.

James Okay.

Lauren Just . . . um . . .

She takes him by the arm and leads him over to a different spot in the room.

This is um. You're . . . um. You're in an armchair. You're reading.

James nods and pretends to be studying an invisible newspaper. Lauren walks back over to Theresa and Marty and Schultz.

Um.

Lauren taps Marty on the shoulder.

Will you be my mom?

Marty nods, smiling. Lauren leads her to a spot in the room across from James.

(*To Marty.*) You're um . . .
You're angry.

Marty Why am I angry?

Lauren Um . . . because he's angry?

A confused pause.

James Should I just . . .

Lauren You should / just –

James Wait – what you said before? About / the –

Lauren Yeah.

Marty Why don't we start? And Lauren . . . you can stop us at any time.

Lauren nods, then steps back. Silence.

Neil.

James continues reading his invisible newspaper.

Neil. I need to talk to you about something.

A pause while James studies his invisible newspaper. Then he looks up.

James (*to Marty and Lauren*) I'm sorry. I'm having a little – I'm kind of drawing a blank.

Marty Can you just go off what Lauren told you?

James I don't really . . . I don't really know who this guy is.

Marty . . . Can you try?

James Can I try to *what*?

Marty sighs. A pause.

Never mind.
Start again.

He goes back to reading his newspaper.

Marty James. I mean Neil.
Neil.
I need to talk to you.

James I'm busy.

Marty You're reading the newspaper.

James The newspaper is important to me.

Marty Please pay attention to me, Neil.

After a second, James puts down his newspaper.

James What is it?

Marty I'm lonely.

James Well, fine. I'm lonely too. We're all lonely.

Marty Then why do you ignore us? Why do you insist on . . . why are you always reading at the dinner table? Or watching TV when you should be talking to Lauren?

A pause.

Why don't you engage with me any more?

James You're too neurotic.

Lauren (*from the corner*) He wouldn't say that. I mean, he wouldn't think that.

Marty What would he think / was –

Lauren He would say that she's always nagging him.

James (*to Marty*) You're always nagging me.

Marty Maybe I'm nagging you because you're ignoring me!

James stands up.

James Maybe I'm ignoring you because you're driving me crazy!

A pause.

Marty Then leave, Neil.
Why don't you just leave?

Another pause.

James I'm stuck.

Marty Well, I'm stuck, too.

James And I, uh . . .

He is in pain. A long pause.

Marty But what about Lauren? Just because you're mad at me doesn't mean you should . . . You can still be nice to your daughter!

Another pause.

James (*softly*) I'm worried she's going to judge me.

Marty She's not going to judge you. She loves you.

James I'm worried she's going to . . .

James starts rubbing the spot between his eyes. It's unclear whether or not he's going to start crying.

I, uh . . .

Marty What? Be straightforward for once!

James . . . I feel ashamed.

Marty Of what?

James Of what I've . . .

A long pause.

. . . Of my life.

Marty But Lauren isn't judging you, Neil.

Pause.

She just wants you to love her.
Neil. Look at me.

James looks up, tears in his eyes.

Lauren just wants you to love her and pay attention to her.

Pause.

That's all you need to do.

After a while, James nods. He and Marty look at each other sadly. After a while Marty breaks and looks at Lauren.

Well?

Lauren purses her lips, thinking. Everyone waits nervously for her response. After a long silence:

Lauren That was pretty good.

Blackout.

FOUR

Breaktime.
Theresa is alone, drinking from her Nalgene. The door opens. It's Schultz. He sees her, sees that she's the only one in the room, and then darts away, shutting the door behind him. Theresa sighs. The door opens again. It's James.

Theresa Hi.

James Hi.

James steps into the room and shuts the door behind him.

. . . That was intense.

Theresa Yeah.

A pause.

You got / pretty –

James I got kind of worked up.

Theresa I mean, I think that's great. Maybe that's what Lauren needed.

James Yeah.

Theresa She's a really sweet kid.

James Yeah. She reminds me of my daughter. In some . . . in certain ways.

Theresa Erin?

James Yeah. Good memory.

Theresa Oh God. I never forget stuff like that. I mean, about people that I . . . people that I find interesting.

Pause.

My ex-boyfriend . . . I like totally memorised his entire life. I'd bring up some girl he kissed in high school and he'd be like: 'Who?' and I'd be like: 'Lopie Grossman, you made out with her twenty years ago,' and he'd be like –
    Jesus. That's actually her name.
    See? I still remember.

James That's amazing.

Theresa It's actually horrible.

Pause.

I'm like haunted by these . . .

A pause.

James So are you and Schultz . . . ?

Theresa Oh. No.
    Yeah. No.

James Huh.

Pause.

Theresa We were. For a little while. I mean, we went out on a / couple of –

James Yeah. I mean, I knew that.

Pause.

Theresa That was a . . . I feel like such an asshole. It was a mistake and now . . . and now things are really weird. I shouldn't be talking to you about it.

Theresa glances towards the door.

James He said that you were still hung up on Mark?

Theresa Schultz said that?

James Yeah.

Theresa So / he –

James He called me and Marty the other night. He was really upset. He hadn't heard back from you and / he –

Theresa Oh God. That's . . .
Oh God. Poor Schultz. I'm such a . . .

She shakes her head.

James What?

Theresa It's just . . . I mean, I *am* really screwed up about Mark. But it's like . . . I mean . . . I would . . . I would like to be, to try being in a relationship right now, you know?

Pause.

Just not with Schultz.
Oh God. I hate myself.

James You shouldn't hate yourself.

Pause.

Was it . . . did you feel like he was too old for you?

63

Theresa Oh. God. No. I always date older guys.

An awkward silence. Theresa goes back to drinking her Nalgene. James watches her.

James You shouldn't hate yourself.

Theresa smiles at him.

Theresa Aw. James. Well . . . thanks.
You're really cool.

James looks down.

You and Marty are like the coolest couple ever. I loved hearing all your . . . your stories and . . . it made me really happy. I was just like: this couple is so cool!

James Yeah. She –

Lauren enters.

Lauren Hi.

Theresa Hey, Lauren.

James nods. Lauren goes over to the corner, sits down, riffles through her backpack, and pulls out a wrapped sandwich. She slowly opens the sandwich and begins eating it, while curiously looking over at James and Theresa. They are self-conscious. After a while:

Theresa So tell me about Erin!

James Oh. Ah . . .

James rubs his forehead.

Theresa How old is she?

James She's twenty-three.

Theresa Okay. Cool.

James She actually ah . . . she refuses . . . she's refusing to, ah, *speak* to me right now.

Lauren, still in the corner, stops chewing. James clears his throat.

Theresa Oh no. Um . . . can I ask / why –

James Marty, ah . . .

He shakes his head.

I guess it's not really Marty's fault.

Theresa Uh-huh.

James Ah . . .

He lowers his voice.

About two months ago, she – Marty – told her something I wish she hadn't . . . Marty didn't – I don't know why she – but Marty didn't realise that Erin . . . That I hadn't told Erin about, ah . . . this ah . . . this, ah . . .

His voice drops even lower and quieter.

. . . very minor infidelity that I, ah, committed during my marriage to, ah, Erin's mother –

Theresa Oh. Okay.

James And ah . . . anyway Marty sort of brought it up on the phone in this sort of casual – I don't know *why* she – but that's beside the – and Erin said: 'Who's Luisa?'

Theresa Oh. God.

James And now she's not speaking to me.

Theresa Oh James.

James She is speaking to Marty.

Theresa Well. That makes sense.

James Yeah. Ah . . . does it?

Theresa I'm sorry.

James Yeah. I just ah . . .

Theresa It'll get better.

James nods. Lauren chews her sandwich and stares at them from her spot in the corner.
Blackout.

FIVE

They are all lying on the floor again. The lights are dimmed.

Theresa One.

James Two.

Silence.

Marty Three.

Schultz Four.

Silence.

Five.

Silence.

Lauren Six.

Marty Seven.

Silence.

James Eight.

Theresa / Schultz Nine.

A very long, disappointed silence.

James One.

Silence.

Lauren Two.

Silence.

66

Schultz Three.

Silence.

Marty Four.

Lauren (*still lying on her back*) I don't get it. I don't get what the point is.

Marty Lauren, maybe you should wait until after class to talk to me about this.

Lauren sits up abruptly.

Lauren (*to Theresa*) You were like a real actress. Why aren't you the teacher?

Still lying down, Theresa shuts her eyes and shakes her head.

What's the point of counting to ten?!

Marty The point is being able to be totally present. To not get in your head and second-guess yourself. Or the people around you.

Lauren I want to know how to become a good *actress.*

Marty That is how you become a good actress.

Theresa She's right, Lauren.

Lauren looks at Theresa, wounded. After a few seconds she lies back down. A long silence.

One.

James Two.

Silence.

Lauren Three.

Marty / Schultz Four.

Blackout.

Week Five

*Marty, centre stage, is facing the audience. She has a tiny
Band-Aid on her forehead. Everyone else sits downstage,
facing Marty.*

Marty My name is Lauren Zadick-White.
   I'm sixteen.
   I was born right before midnight, on October 24th.
Um . . . I'm a Scorpio, and my mother says that accounts
for why I'm such a hard worker.
   Also why I'm so stubborn!
   Ah . . . this fall I'll be a junior at Shirley High. School
is okay, but I can't wait to go to college and start doing
what I love, which is theatre and dance. I'm also really
interested in going to veterinary school. We'll see. I don't
have to make any decisions right now, even though I
think I do.

   She gazes pointedly at Lauren.

I don't enjoy talking that much about my family and my,
um, background, but it's actually fascinating and just . . .
really, really interesting.
   My mother is Lebanese, and my father is Irish. Both of
them were born outside of the States and they met at the
University of Iowa.
   Um . . . my grandmother lives with us. We call her
'Sitti'. That's Lebanese for 'Grandma'. I'm really close
with her. Everyone says we look alike.

   Pause.

I have agreed to let all of you know that in the past
couple of years my father has had some problems with

68

the, um, law. I hope that this will remain strictly confidential. It has been really hard for my whole family, especially my mother and grandmother, who have always had such high expectations. My grandmother thinks my mother should leave my father. They fight about it.

Pause.

I'm not going to go into any more detail.

Pause.

It is really hard for me to talk about it and I should be so proud of myself for sharing it with all of you.

Pause.

Oh. Also. This fall they're doing *West Side Story* at the high school and I would really like to get the part of Maria. It's my dream role. I signed up for this class so I would be, um, better prepared for it.

Pause.

I hope that I . . .
Maybe one day I can stop putting so much pressure on myself.

Blackout.

TWO

James and Lauren and Marty are watching Theresa and Schultz, who stand in the centre of the room facing each other.

Theresa I want it.

Schultz You can't have it.

Silence.

Theresa I want it.

Schultz You can't have it.

Theresa I WANT IT.

Schultz You can't have it.

Theresa I WANT IT.

Schultz You can't have it.

Marty Come on, Schultz. Really get into it.

Theresa I want it.

Schultz Well, you can't have it.

Theresa But I want it.

Schultz You can't have it.

Theresa I FUCKING WANT IT!

Silence.

Schultz Jesus.

*Schultz wipes his mouth with his sleeve, a little upset.
He puts his hands on his hips.*

(*Shaking his head.*) You can't have it.

Marty Switch phrases.

Theresa I want to go.

Schultz . . . Wait, what do I say?

Marty 'I need you to stay.'

Schultz I need you to stay.

Theresa Well, I want to go.

Schultz regards Theresa sadly.

Schultz I need you to stay.

Theresa I want to go.

Schultz I need you to stay.

Theresa But I / want to –

Schultz I need you to stay.

After a short pause.

I need you to stay.

Marty Good.

Theresa I want to go.

Schultz I. Need. You. To. Stay.

Theresa I want to go.

Schultz steps forward and grabs Theresa by the shoulders.

Schultz I NEED YOU TO STAY.

Marty Okay, no touching.

Theresa I want to go.
(*To Marty.*) I'm sorry. I need to go the bathroom.
(*To James.*) Will you step in for me?

James . . . Sure.

Theresa exits quickly. Schultz and James stand facing each other.
   Blackout.

THREE

Lauren and James are standing, facing each other. Theresa is hovering nearby, watching them. Schultz and Marty are leaning against the mirrors.

Lauren Stop haunting me, Mark.

A pause.

James You shouldn't have broken up with me.
You made a mistake.

Lauren No I didn't.

James Yes you did.

Lauren No I didn't. You were domineering and you
made me feel . . . you made forget Who I Am.

James Who cares? Now you're going to be alone for ever.

Lauren No I'm not.

James Yes you are.

Lauren No I'm not.

James Yes you are.

Lauren No I'm not.

James Yes you are.

Silence.

Lauren No I'm not.

Marty *(from the corner)* Okay. Let's make it a little /
more –

Lauren I'm not going to be alone for ever.

James I'm the best guy you'll ever have, Theresa. I was
the best guy you'll ever have.

Lauren You don't know that. Have you . . . have you,
like, met all the guys in the world?

Pleased with herself, Lauren glances over at Theresa.

James No one will ever love you the way that I do.

Lauren You were too possessive.

James That was one of the things you secretly liked about me.

Lauren (*glancing over at Theresa*) No it wasn't?

Theresa shakes her head.

Yes it was. Okay, yes it was, but that doesn't mean it was good for me. I am a beautiful um really cool woman and I'm really attractive and there are lots of men out there who will like me and be nice to me.

James You're fooling yourself.

A pause. Lauren sighs.

Lauren I don't know what I'm supposed to say.

Theresa speaks up from the corner.

Theresa I don't want to be with a man who threatens me.

James I'm not threatening you. I'm telling you the truth.

Theresa (*stepping forward*) No. That's not . . . it's because you're insecure, Mark. You could never just let me love you and be free. You were so . . . you were so judgmental and moralistic. You were always lecturing me. If you really love someone, you don't make them feel bad about themselves! All this negative stuff you're saying . . . it's just . . . it's just further proof that you don't really care about me the way that you say you do. If you really loved me, you'd want me to feel okay about the future. You'd want me to be optimistic.

Silence. Then James smiles.

James I'm speechless.

Theresa grins.

Theresa Whew!

Marty That was great.

Lauren (*to Theresa*) Sorry.

Theresa No! You were awesome.

Lauren (*to Marty*) He was starting to make me feel really bad.

Theresa gives James a high five.

Theresa That was so crazy, man! You totally reminded me of him!

James beams. Schultz watches all of this, expressionless. Blackout.

FOUR

Breaktime.
Marty is alone in the room, standing in front of the mirrors, looking at her reflection and fussing a little with the Band-Aid on her forehead. After a while Schultz enters. He looks at her.

Schultz What happened?

Marty Oh. God. Yeah. It's . . . I fell out of bed. Two nights ago. If you can believe it.

Schultz Why?

Marty . . . Why what?

Schultz Why did you fall out of bed?

Marty Oh. Um . . . I don't know. I'm not sure what happened. I just woke up and I was on the floor. It's happened to me a bunch of times in the past couple of years.

Schultz Are you a restless sleeper?

Marty Um –

Schultz Do you talk a lot? Wake up screaming?

Marty Well, James says I do. And the other week / I –

Schultz Night terrors.

Marty What?

Schultz You probably have night terrors.

Marty smiles.

It's a real thing, Marty.

Marty What is it?

Schultz Becky used to get them. They're uh . . . they're different from dreams because they're just . . . they're just fear. And they can make you have these like, these little seizures. And sometimes you fall out of bed.

Marty Huh.

Schultz Were you abused as a child?

Marty I'm sorry?

Schultz Were you abused as a child?

Marty . . . No. Um. No. I don't think so.

Schultz Okay. 'Cause it's a common symptom among abuse survivors.

Marty Huh.

Pause.

Schultz Night terrors.

Marty Huh. Yeah. Maybe. I don't know what it was.

Schultz It was night terrors.

Marty Yeah.

Schultz Becky went on medications for . . . She went on some kind of epilepsy medication. It helped her.

Marty Huh.

Pause.

And it's a real –

Schultz It's a real thing. It's a real thing. Look it up online.

Marty Okay. Yeah. Thanks.

Silence.

How're you doing, Schultz? Are you okay?

Pause.

Schultz Uh . . . I don't know.

Pause.

How are you?

James suddenly enters, exuberant, with a bottle of water.

James I hooped.
I hooped for over a minute.

Marty . . . Wow. Great.

James Now Theresa is giving Lauren a massage. In the parking lot. It's hilarious. You guys should go take a look.

Marty and Schultz both attempt to smile.

Marty . . . That's great.

James suddenly grabs Marty in his arms and gives her a kiss. It's a little awkward. Marty smiles at Schultz, embarrassed.
Blackout.

FIVE

The entire group is sitting in a circle.

Marty When I go to India . . . I'm going to bring my purple shawl.

Lauren Wait. I've played this before. Isn't it California? 'When I go to California'? We played this in fifth grade.

Marty This time we're playing it with India. When I go to India I will bring my purple shawl. Schultz?

Schultz I don't understand / what –

Lauren Say what she said and then add something.

After a pause.

'When I go to India I'm gonna bring my purple shawl and a' – like another object. Then the next person lists all the other things and adds on something new.

Schultz Ah . . . when I go to India I'm gonna bring my purple shawl and ah . . .

A long silence.

Marty Whatever you want.

Another long silence.

Schultz Phillips-head screwdriver.

Marty Okay.

Lauren When I go to India I'm gonna bring a purple shawl and a Phillips-head screwdriver and a . . . a toothbrush.

Marty Theresa! Quick! And get creative!

Theresa When I go to India I'm going to bring a purple shawl and a Phillips-head screwdriver and a toothbrush and . . . a tiny velvet cape.

Lauren *What?*

Theresa Sorry. Just a cape. A velvet cape.

Marty Good! Keep going! James!

James When I go to India I'm gonna bring a . . . a . . . a purple shawl and a Phillips-head screwdriver and a toothbrush and a velvet cape and . . . ah . . . the Bible.

Marty
WhenIgotoIndiaI'mgonnabringapurpleshawlandaPhillips headscrewdriverandatoothbrushandavelvetcapeandacopy oftheBibleand . . . a bottle of red wine!

Pause.

Schultz!

Schultz Okay.
I can do this.

Pause.

When I go to India I'm gonna bring a purple shawl and a Phillips-head screwdriver and a toothbrush and a and a and a and a copy of the Bible and a . . . and a big ol' bottle of red wine! Yes! Oh. And a battle axe!

A long pause.

Lauren You forgot the velvet cape.

Schultz . . . I did?

A pause.

Marty Did he?
Who remembers?

Lauren He forgot.

James I didn't notice.

Marty Me neither.

*A silence, during which Theresa grapples with an
ethical dilemma. Finally:*

Theresa Um . . . I think he forgot.

A wounded silence.

Marty Okay. Um. Schultz, you're out.

Schultz What does that mean?

Marty You're just . . .
You have to leave the circle.

*After a while Schultz gets up. He stands there for a few
seconds, then walks away from the circle. He wavers
on his feet, clenching and unclenching his fists.*

Whose turn is it?

Lauren Me. Um . . . When I go to India I'm gonna bring
a purple ca— a purple shawl, a Phillips-head screwdriver,
a toothbrush . . .

*While Lauren is talking Schultz walks over to the wall
of mirrors and stands there, making direct eye contact
with his own reflection. He remains there, unmoving.*

. . . a velvet cape, a copy of the Bible . . . a bottle of red
wine . . . and um . . . a battle axe. And a calico kitten.

Pause.

I did it! Right? I did it!

*Marty, who has been glancing over in Schultz's
direction, clears her throat.*

Marty You know what? I want us to try something
different.

Lauren But –

Schultz (*still facing his reflection, not moving*) It's fine,
Marty.

Marty No. No. I . . . I just forgot how competitive this game is. And it's . . . this . . . what we're doing in this class is really not about competition.

Silence.

Schultz.
   Please come back and join us in the circle.

Schultz slowly turns around and rejoins the circle.

Great. So this next exercise is . . . Hm. Wait. We need paper.

Marty gets up and hurries over to her backpack. She takes out a flyer and hurries back into the circle. She begins tearing the flyer into five strips.

Okay. We're going to . . . uhp. You know what? We also need pencils.

She gets up again and hurries back over to her backpack, then rummages through it. They all watch her.

I've got one . . . two . . . three . . . this is useable, I guess . . . four . . .

James I've got a pen.

Marty Okay. Perfect.

She returns to the circle.

So. Everyone take a . . .

Marty hands out the pencils/pens.

Okay. So I want everyone to take your scrap of paper and write on it . . . I want you to write down a secret that you've never, ever told *anyone*.

Lauren Whoa.

Marty And . . . you don't have to be specific. We don't need to know it's you. In fact, we *shouldn't* know it's you. This is an opportunity to have people . . . to be able to air a secret in front of a group without feeling like you have to . . . like you have to answer to it. Or someone.

Silence.

Theresa What if we don't have any secrets?

Marty You must have *one*.

Theresa I don't know. I've been pretty open in all my relationships. I basically tell my partners everything.

Marty Okay. Well, if you can't – just try to think of something that . . . something that's hard for you to talk about.

Theresa nods.

Okay. So. Just . . . don't take too long. Write down the first big thing that comes into your mind. Even if it's scary.

They all nod.

All right. Go for it.

Everyone (including Marty) starts writing/thinking/ chewing on their pens/scootching away to a different part of the floor to have the right amount of privacy to write/think/chew on their pens. Silence and then the sound of scribbling for about forty-five seconds.

Is everyone done?

Lauren Just . . . hold on.

Schultz Yeah. I need a few more seconds.

Marty waits for about ten more seconds.

Marty Okay. Now fold up your paper into four – fold it twice into a little square and give it back to me.

They all obey.

And let's all sit together again.

They return to the circle.

Okay.

She takes the little pieces of paper and shakes them in her cupped hands

. . . We're each gonna pick one. And we're gonna stand in front of the group and read it silently to ourselves, and then we're gonna read it out loud to the group. In a very sincere . . . in a meaningful way.

Schultz What if you pick your own?

Marty Just read it anyway. We won't know.

Pause.

Okay?
Trust me, guys.
Lauren.
Pick one.

Lauren picks a square of paper.

Marty Okay . . . now . . .

She hands the papers out.

Schultz . . .
James . . .
Theresa . . .
Okay.
And I guess this one is for me.

Pause.

Um . . . Schultz. Can you stand up?

Schultz stands up.

Will you deliver your secret, please?

Schultz opens his piece of paper, reads it silently, and then looks up.

Schultz My father may have molested me.

A slightly shocked silence.

Marty Okay. Thank you.

Schultz sits down.

Theresa?

Theresa stands up. She unfolds and looks at her piece of paper.

Theresa I secretly think I am smarter than everyone else in the world.

A pause. Lauren giggles.

Marty Lauren.
Great, Theresa. Good job.

Theresa sits back down.

James?

James slowly stands up, unfolds and then reads directly from his paper.

James I have a problempossibleaddiction –

He looks up.

that's written as one word –
with internet pornography.

Lauren covers her mouth with her hand.

Marty Great. Thank you.

James sits back down.

Lauren?

Lauren stands up. She reads her paper, then stuffs it into her pocket. She looks out at the group.

Lauren I think I might be in love with Theresa.

A very long silence. Lauren is still standing.

Um . . .

Marty You can sit down. Thank you.

Lauren sits down. Another horrible ten-second silence. Schultz frowns, then looks traumatised, then stares angrily at James, then looks traumatised again.

Okay. Ah . . . I guess it's my turn.

Marty stands up. She unfolds her piece of paper and reads it out loud, not taking her eyes off the paper. Her voice is shaky.

Sometimes I think that everything I do is propelled by my fear of being alone.

A very long silence. Marty finally crumples the paper in her fist. She refuses to make eye contact with anyone.

Great job, you guys.

Blackout.

SIX

They are all lying on their backs in the semi-darkness. Silence for a while.

Marty (*dully*) Okay. Next week is our last class. So let's really try to . . .

A long silence.

Lauren One.

Silence.

James Two.

Silence.

Lauren Three.

Silence.

Theresa Four.

James Five.

A long silence.

Schultz Six.

Silence.

James Seven.

Theresa Eight.

Marty Nine.

A very very long silence.

Lauren Ten.

No one moves.
Blackout.

Week Six

ONE

The room, in darkness. The sound of footsteps in the hallway. Marty enters the room, her bag over her shoulder, and turns on the lights. She stands there for a while, tired. She walks over to the corner of the room and puts her bag down.

She walks over to the yoga ball, and sits down. She bounces there, sadly, for about fifteen seconds.

The door opens. James enters.

Marty stops bouncing.

James walks over to the corner and puts his bag down. He stands there in the corner, looking at her. She stays on the ball and looks at him. They look at each other for a while.

Marty You came.

James Of course.

She nods. Silence for a while.

I talked to Erin the other night. Finally.

Marty nods.

She said you didn't call her back this week. That she left you / five –

Marty So that's good. So you talked to each other.

He nods. More silence.

James How's Phyllis?

Marty Fine.

Silence.

James So what are you . . .
  Are you on the *couch* / or –

Marty There's an air mattress.

  More silence.

James Come home, Marty.

Marty No fucking way.

  Another silence.

James You . . . did you want this to happen or something?

Marty Did I *what*?

James Having us write out –
  Did you *want* me / to –

Marty Okay. See. That's exactly. That's exactly the problem.
  That right there.

  The door opens. It's Schultz, with his backpack.

Schultz Hi, guys.

James Hey, Schultz.

  Schultz steps inside and starts putting his backpack down in the corner.

Schultz How were your – Did you guys have a good week?

  Marty and James both nod. Awkward silence for a little while. Schultz unzips his backpack and takes out a little box.

Ah . . . Marty?

Marty Mmhm?

Schultz I wanted to, uh . . .

87

Schultz walks over to Marty and hands her the little box.

. . . Thanks.

Marty Oh, Schultz.

Schultz For everything. It's been a great class.

Marty looks down at the box.

Marty Should I –

Schultz Yeah. Open it.

Marty rips off the paper and takes the lid off the box.

Marty Oh wow.

She stares at the box's contents.

Schultz Yep.

Marty This is really great.

Schultz Do you already have one?

Marty Um . . . well, yes, I do, but it's bigger, and not as nice. It's in the living room.

James (*from across the room*) What is it?

Schultz It's a dream-catcher.

Marty We can put this one . . . I can put this one in the . . .

Marty trails off. She lifts the dream-catcher out of the box and holds it up to the light.

I love the little purple –

Schultz Ah man. I was hoping you didn't already have one.

Marty No. No. I love it. I love it.

Marty puts it back in the box.

Schultz The Native Americans used them to uh . . .

An awkward silence. He has forgotten.

Marty Thank you so much, Schultz.

Schultz Maybe it'll help with the night terrors.

Marty Mmhm.

Schultz Night-terror catcher.

Schultz looks at James.

Did she tell you about those?

James shakes his head.
Blackout.

TWO

They are all sitting in a circle.

Marty If

Lauren I

Schultz Wanted

Theresa To

James Become

Marty A

Lauren . . . Actress

Schultz I

Theresa Would

James Just

Marty Go

Lauren (*pause*) Home.

Schultz . . . I

Theresa Have

James Learned

Marty So

Lauren Um . . . Much.

Schultz (*pause*) I

Theresa Will

James Try

Marty To

Lauren Realise

Schultz The

Theresa Gigantic-ness!

James Of

Marty Capabilities!

Lauren And

Schultz The

Theresa Way

James I

Marty Express

Lauren Anger

Schultz Is

Theresa . . . Indescribable.

James Peace

Marty Is

Lauren Just

Schultz Okay

Theresa For

James Everybody

Marty But

Lauren We

Schultz Will

Theresa Succeed

James Always

Marty If

Lauren We

Schultz Try

Theresa And

James Become

Marty . . . Flowers.

Silence.

That was perfect.

Blackout.

THREE

They are all sitting in a circle.

Lauren Okay. Um.

I was on the subway. In New York. And there was this old guy. Who was . . . who was maybe Jewish.

He had a beard.
A-and . . .

A pause.

He was totally anti-Semitic.

Lauren sighs.

Marty It's okay, Lauren.

Lauren I don't remember anything else.

Lauren sits back down.

Marty Does anyone else remember something from the first day?

A pause. No one says anything.

Okay. Well. I think maybe we'll do one more exercise and then / call it a –

Schultz Wait! I do.

Schultz stands up. He clears his throat.

Uh . . . okay.
I was at a wedding.
In, ah . . . Eureka, California.
Right near the Oregon border. Where there are a lot of redwoods. It's really beautiful up there.
This is nineteen-eighty . . . something.
There was this big wedding. Two of my friends were getting married in this big old hotel. And we . . . uh . . . we were all sleeping on straw mats. In the lobby. Of the hotel.
We were all drunk.
And we'd been dancing.
And uh . . . there was this guy. I'd been looking at this guy all night. This really attractive, really beautiful guy who just . . . who caught my attention. But I didn't think

anything would happen because he was just surrounded by women. All the women liked him.

Pause.

He was one of those guys. Those guys that get all the women.

Pause.

Then I was getting ready to go to sleep on my straw mat and I noticed that he was sitting . . . that he was lying next to me. On his straw mat. And even though they'd turned off all the lights I could tell that he was looking at me.
And I felt . . .
I felt seen. And he smiled at me. I could feel him smiling in the dark.
And then I smiled back.
And neither of us had to say anything, because we knew that we would spend the / rest –

Marty Schultz?

Schultz – of our lives together.

Marty That was great. Thank you.

Schultz I'm not finished.

Marty The thing is . . . it's quarter till, and I want to make sure we can squeeze in the last exercise.

Schultz . . . Oh. Okay.

Silence.

Theresa That was beautiful, Schultz.

Schultz can't quite bear to look at Theresa, but he nods.

Schultz Yeah. Thanks.

Blackout.

FOUR

Schultz and Lauren stand in the centre of the stage, facing each other. Marty, James and Theresa watch from the wall.

Schultz (*to Marty*) Five years?

Marty Ten years. Ten years from now.

Schultz takes a deep breath.

Schultz Okay.

Schultz walks away from Lauren, then turns around and feigns surprise.

Lauren?

Lauren Yeah?

Schultz Is that you?!

Lauren Yeah. Hi, Schultz.

Schultz Hey!

Silence.

What are you doing here in . . . Burlington?

Lauren Um . . . I live here now.

Schultz Weird. So do I!

Pause.

I live here with my wife.

Lauren You got married again?

Schultz Yeah. Yeah. She's fantastic.

Lauren That's so cool.

Pause.

What's her name?

Schultz Ah . . . Susan.
Yeah.
She's a, uh . . .
She's a seamstress.

Lauren Wow.

Silence.

Schultz How are you?

Lauren I'm, um, I'm okay.

Schultz How old are you now?

Lauren I'm . . .

A pause while she calculates.

. . . twenty-six.

Schultz Oh. Man. That's awesome.

Silence.

Lauren I live here with my boyfriend.

Schultz Aw. Great.

Lauren Todd.

Schultz That's great.

Lauren He's a, um . . . he's a doctor. Veterinarian.
We run a veterinary clinic together.

Schultz What happened to acting?

Lauren Oh. Yeah.

Schultz I thought you wanted to be an actress.

Lauren No. I . . . I did a lot of acting in college. I was,
like . . . I starred in a lot of . . . but now I'm a veterinarian.

Schultz That's great.

Lauren I really like it.

Silence.

Schultz So you're happy?

Lauren Yeah. I think so.

Schultz Yeah.

Lauren Are you happy?

Schultz I am. I am. I'm very happy. Susan is just . . . she's changed my life around. And business is going really well.

Lauren Are you still making your chairs?

Schultz Oh yeah. Oh yeah.

Pause.

Have you heard from any of the others?

Lauren Oh. Um –

Schultz Do you know how Theresa is doing?

Marty opens her mouth and starts to step forward to interrupt them, but Theresa stops her.

Lauren Um. Yeah.

She glances over at Theresa.

She's like a really successful massage therapist. In Putney.

Schultz Oh, that's good.

Lauren Yeah. And she married this like actor. He's kind of famous.

Theresa giggles from the wall.

Lauren I forget his name. He's really good-looking.

Schultz Huh. That's good.

Pause.

Man. She really screwed with my head.

Lauren . . . Yeah.

Schultz But ah . . . I don't really think about her that much any more.

Lauren Yeah.

Schultz Have you heard from Marty or James?

Over the next thirty seconds, the lights fade so that Marty, James and Theresa eventually disappear, and only Lauren and Schultz remain, in a spotlight.

Lauren Um . . . yeah. A couple of years ago. I got um . . . I got like a Christmas card from Marty.

Schultz What'd she say?

Lauren Oh. She um. She moved to New Mexico.

Schultz Oh wow.

Lauren Yeah. She started some kind of like arts programme? For poor kids? Some kind of like drama thing?

Schultz Huh.

Lauren Yeah. She lives in Taos. In this really beautiful, um, adobe hut. She sent me a picture.

Schultz So you two kept in touch.

Lauren Yeah. A little. I got . . . It's funny. I didn't get the lead in *West Side Story* that fall, but I got the, um . . . I got the part of Anita? Which was actually –

Schultz Aw. I wish I'd known.

Lauren Yeah. I called Marty and told her. She came to see it.

Silence.

Schultz So she and James aren't together any more?

Lauren shakes her head.

Do you know where / he –

Lauren I think he's still in Shirley. At the college.
Teaching economics.

Schultz Huh.

Silence.

How's your family?

Lauren Oh. Um . . . my parents got divorced this past
fall.
Yeah.
After um . . . after thirty years of marriage.

Schultz I'm so sorry.

Lauren Yeah. No. I mean, I think it was a good decision.

An awkward silence.

Hey. Um. This is kind of a weird – but do you ever
wonder how many times your life is gonna end?

A pause.

Schultz Uh . . . I'm not sure I know what / you –

Lauren Like how many people you're . . . like how many
times your life is gonna totally change and then, like, start
all over again? And you'll feel like what happened before
wasn't real and what's happening now is actually . . . (*She
trails off.*)

Schultz Uh . . . I don't know. I guess I feel like my life is
pretty real.

Lauren . . . Yeah.

Silence.

Schultz Well. Uh. It's great seeing you.

Lauren Yeah. You too.

Schultz I always really liked you, Lauren.

Lauren Yeah. I liked you too.

They smile awkwardly at each other and do not move. Then, perhaps, very faintly, we hear the sounds of a street in Burlington: people talking, a car honking, plates clinking at an outdoor restaurant.
  The spotlight goes out.
  End of play.